THE POST OFFICE

David and Patricia Armentrout

Rourke
Publishing LLC
Vero Beach, Florida 32964

www.rourkepublishing.com

PHOTO CREDITS: © christine balderas: title page; © Naomi Bassitt: page 4; © 344512847: page 5; © Michelle Malven: page 6 left; ©Steve Snyder: page 6 right; © USPS: page 7, 8, 10, 15, 22; © Armentrout: page 9, 12, 13; © Robert Pernell: page 14; © U.S. Air Force photo/Tech. Sgt. Shane A. Cuomo: page 17; © Leah-Anne Thompson: page 18© Richard Cano: page 19; © Associated Press-BOB DAUGHERTY: page 20; © constantgardener: page 21; © VINCENT GIORDANO: page 23

Editor: Kelli Hicks

Cover and Interior design by Teri Intzegian

Library of Congress Cataloging-in-Publication Data

Armentrout, David, 1962-
  The post office / David and Patricia Armentrout.
      p. cm. -- (Our community)
   ISBN 978-1-60472-340-3
  1. Postal service--Juvenile literature. I. Armentrout, Patricia, 1960- II.
Title.
   HE6078.A76 2009
   383--dc22
                                    2008016347

Printed in the USA

CG/CG

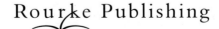

Rourke Publishing

www.rourkepublishing.com – rourke@rourkepublishing.com
Post Office Box 3328, Vero Beach, FL 32964

Table of Contents

The Post Office

Have you ever sent something through the mail? Maybe you're expecting a letter from someone far away. The post office will deliver your mail.

A letter begins its journey
through the postal service.

A Friendly Face

Letter carriers deliver mail to homes and businesses. They meet a lot of people in their community.

Letter carriers usually work the same delivery route everyday.

Letter carriers also collect mail and bring it back to the post office.

Have you seen one of these blue mailboxes in your community?

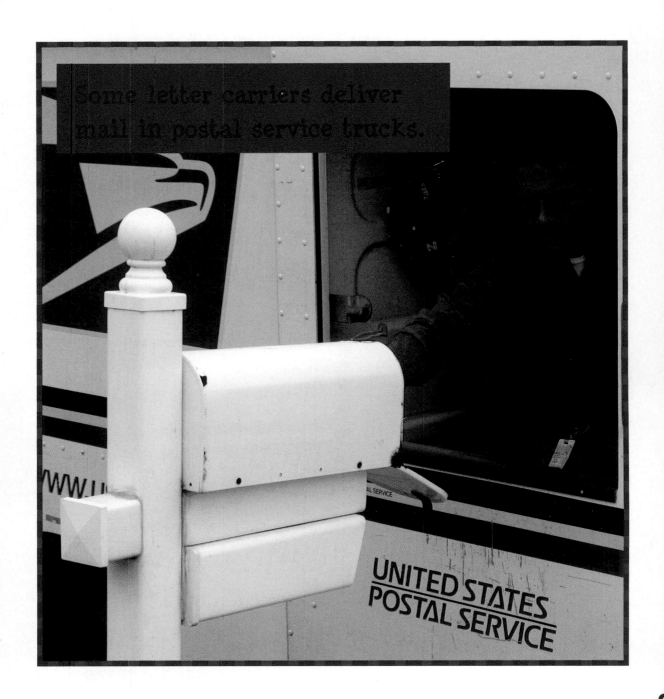

Some letter carriers deliver mail in postal service trucks.

The Lobby

Postal customers can find everything they need in a post office lobby. A lobby has mail drop slots, packaging supplies, and **postage** scales.

A customer weighs a package on a lobby postage scale.

Postage is the cost of mailing something. The amount of postage depends on the size, shape, weight, and time needed for delivery of a package.

A .41¢ stamp

Gerald R. Ford

41 USA

2007

Clerks

Postal clerks work behind a counter. The most important job they have is to help customers. They sell stamps and supplies. They also collect and weigh outgoing mail.

Postal clerks can answer any shipping question a customer has.

The post office sells boxes,
envelopes, labels, and tape.

Processing Mail

A **mail processing center** sorts mail for many communities. Processing centers have machines that sort mail by size and shape.

A cancelled stamp is marked with lines. A cancelled stamp cannot be reused.

A postal employee guides envelopes through a sorting machine.

Trucks move mail from processing centers to local post offices. Mail handlers sort mail for letter carriers.

The post office delivers millions of pieces of mail every delivery day.

A mail handler sorts incoming packages.

Addressing an Envelope

Do you know how to address an envelope? The post office likes everyone to use the same format.

Line 1:   Name

Line 2:   House number and street name

Line 3:   City, State and **ZIP Code**

A ZIP Code is a group of
numbers the post office gives
to a delivery area.

This Space For Writing Messages

POST CARD

Place
Stamp Here

Domestic
One cent

Foreign
Two cents

Rourke Publishing LLC
P.O. Box 643328
Vero Beach, FL 32964-3328

This side for the Address only.

ZIP Code

Moving Mail

The post office uses trucks, cars, boats, and trains to deliver mail. They even deliver by mule to **remote** places like the Havasupai Indian Reservation in Arizona.

People in out-of-the-way places get mail, too!

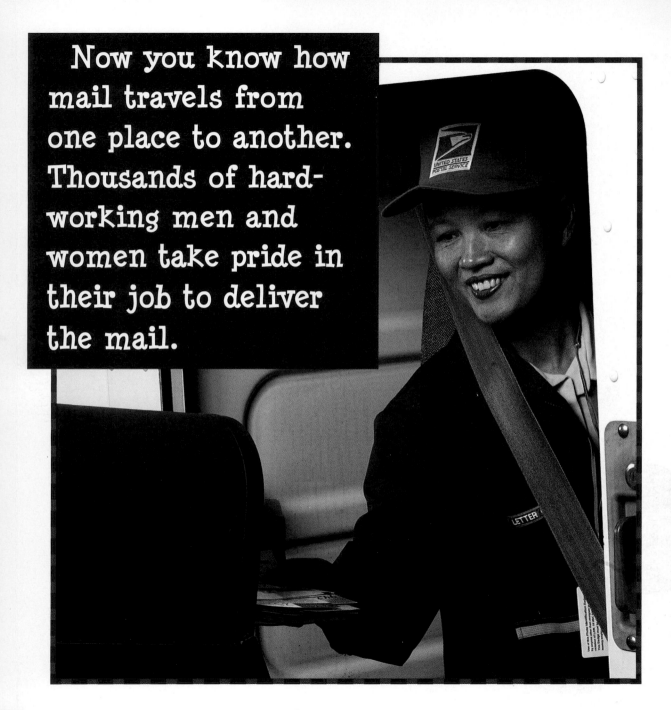

Now you know how mail travels from one place to another. Thousands of hard-working men and women take pride in their job to deliver the mail.

Glossary

mail processing center (MAYL-PROSS-ess-ing): place where mail is sorted for many communities

postage (POH stij): the cost of mailing something

remote (ri-MOHT): far away or hard to reach place

ZIP Code (ZIP-KODE): a numbered code defining an area, or zone, for mailing; Zone Improvement Plan

INDEX

FURTHER READING

Trumbauer, Lisa. *What Does a Mail Carrier Do?* Enslow Elementary, 2005.

Kule, Elaine. *The U.S. Mail*. Enslow Publishers, 2002.

WEBSITES

The United States Postal Service
www.usps.com

National Postal Museum
www.postalmuseum.si.edu

ABOUT THE AUTHORS

David and Patricia Armentrout specialize in nonfiction children's books. They enjoy exploring different topics and have written about many subjects, including sports, animals, history, and people. David and Patricia love to spend their free time outdoors with their two boys and dog Max.